BOOK of SPACE
Questions and Answers

By Rosie McCormick

Contents

Introduction

People have always asked questions about space.
You can find answers to some of your questions
in this book. Scientists have found many answers
to their questions. They have made amazing discoveries,
but there is still much more to explore.

Space

What makes up space?

When you look up at the night sky, you can
see space. Stars, planets and moons fill space.
A star is a ball of gas that gives off light and heat.
A planet is a large object that moves around a star.
A moon is an object that moves around a planet.

Where is our place in space?

We live on Earth which is a planet. Moons move around planets so our Moon moves around Earth. Planets move around stars so Earth moves around the Sun which is a star.

Earth

Stars

What makes the stars shine?

Stars are huge balls of gas that produce heat and light. Most stars look like bright dots because they are so far away.

We cannot see the real colours of stars. Very hot stars are blue. Hot stars are yellow. Cooler stars are red. The hotter a star is, the more brightly it shines.

hot stars

Why do we only see most stars at night?

The Sun is the closest star to Earth. It is so close that it appears very bright. During the day the Sun is so bright that we cannot see other stars. Even though we cannot see the other stars and planets, they are still in space.

What are constellations?

Sometimes people think that the stars form
pictures in the sky. Constellations are
the groups of stars that form these pictures.
Long ago some people gave the star pictures
names such as Scorpion, Southern Cross and Lion.

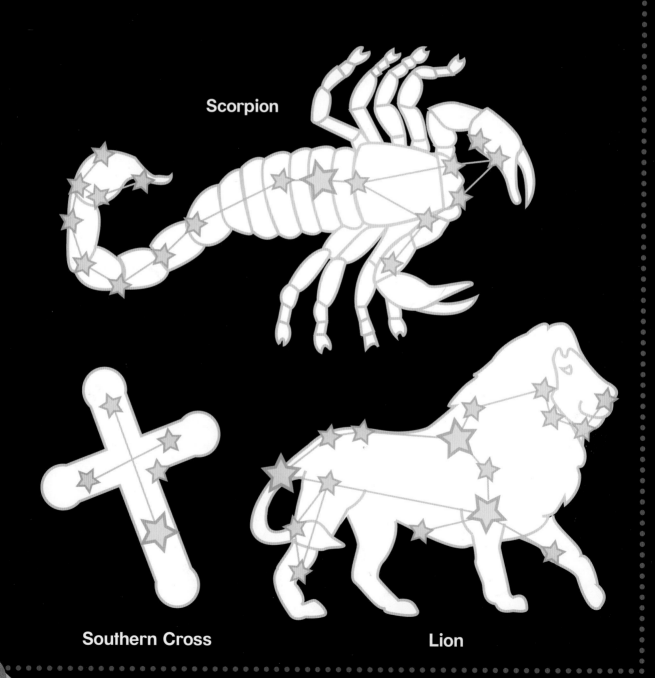

Scorpion

Southern Cross

Lion

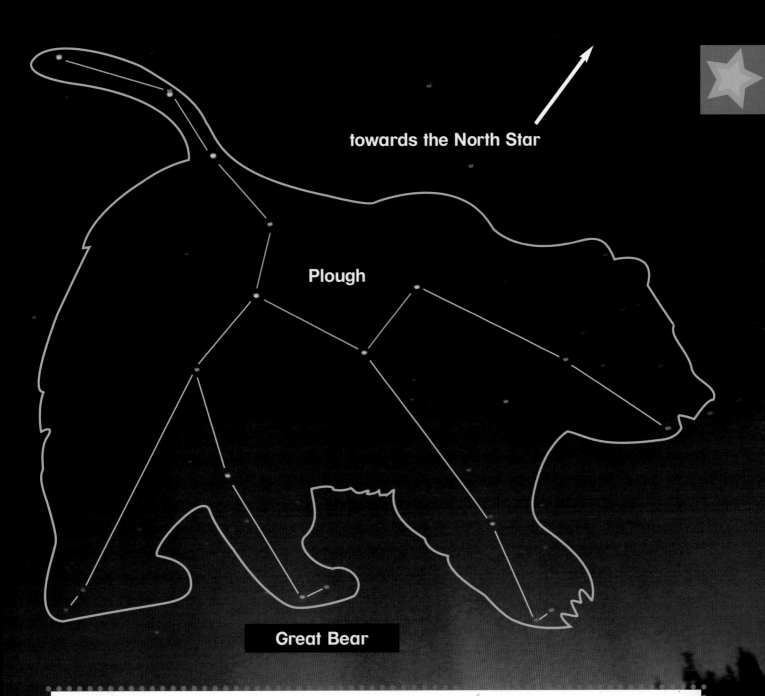

towards the North Star

Plough

Great Bear

How do star gazers use constellations?

Star gazers use constellations to find special stars.
One constellation called the Great Bear has a
smaller group of seven stars called the Plough.
Two bright stars in the Plough help you find
the North Star. Sometimes when people are lost,
they use the North Star to guide them.

9

The Sun

What kind of star is the Sun?

The Sun is a yellow star. It is more than 14 million degrees Celsius in the centre. That is only medium hot for a star. The Sun is much bigger than Earth. More than a million Earths could fit inside our Sun.

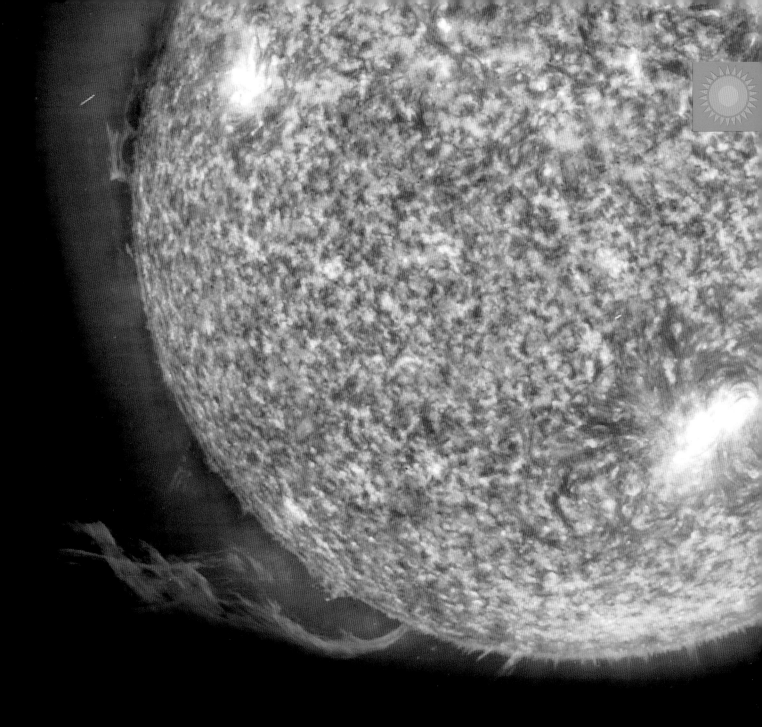

How far away is the Sun?

The Sun is about 150 million kilometres from Earth.
If Earth was closer to the Sun, then it would be
too hot to live on. If Earth was much farther away,
then it would be too cold to live on.

The Moon

What is it like on the Moon?

The Moon has many holes called craters on its surface. There are also mountains on the Moon. Some parts of the Moon are hotter than boiling water. Other parts are colder than ice.

Can people live on the Moon?

Plants and animals need air to breathe and water to drink. There is no air or water on the Moon. To live on the Moon, people must bring air and water with them. So no one can live there.

The Moon has many holes called craters on its surface.

How far away is the Moon?

The Moon is about 383,000 kilometres from Earth. It is our closest neighbour in space. If you could drive to the Moon, it would take months to get there. If you travelled by spacecraft, it would take a few days.

Moon

Earth

How does the Moon shine?

Even though the Moon shines, it has no light of its own. The light from the Moon comes from the Sun. The Sun shines on the Moon just like it shines on Earth. People see the part of the Moon that has the Sun's light shining on it.

light

Sun

Moon

light

Earth

Why does the Moon seem to change shape?

The Moon travels around Earth. As it moves, only the surface that is lit by the Sun can be seen on Earth. This makes it look like the Moon changes shape, but it doesn't. It is always the shape of a ball.

full Moon

quarter Moon

crescent Moon

Our Solar System

What is our solar system?

At the centre of our solar system is the Sun.
Everything moves around it. There are nine
main planets. Many of them have moons.
There are also millions of smaller objects
in our solar system like asteroids and comets.

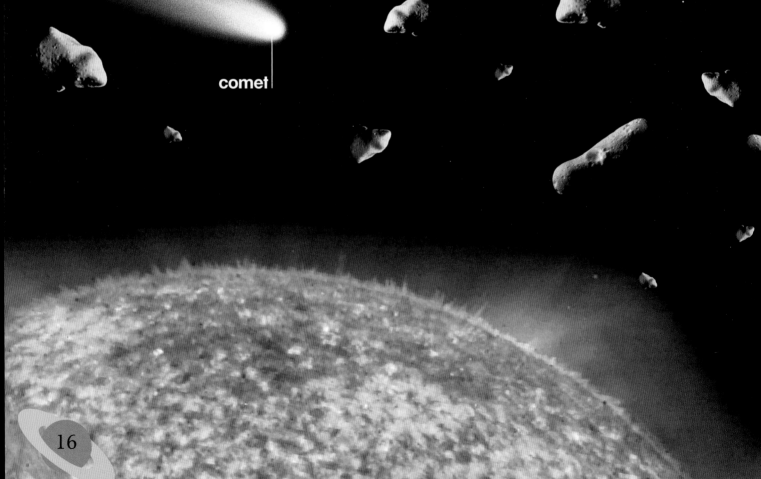

comet

What is an orbit?

An orbit is the path an object takes when it travels around something. When we say a planet "orbits" the Sun, we mean it follows a path around the Sun. All the planets in our solar system orbit the Sun. The Moon orbits Earth. Other moons orbit other planets.

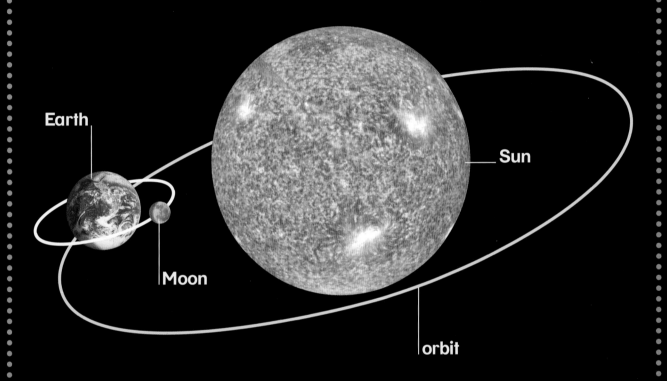

Earth

Sun

Moon

orbit

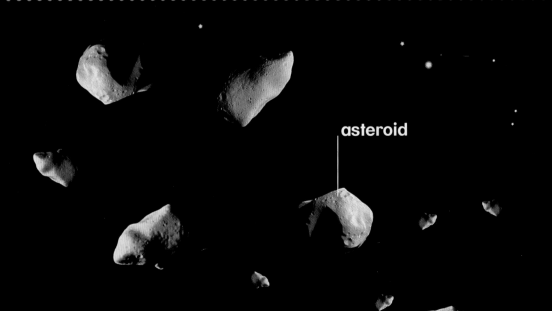

asteroid

What are the planets in our solar system?

Mercury, Venus, Earth, Mars, Jupiter, Saturn, Uranus, Neptune and Pluto are the main planets in our solar system. Pluto is the smallest and Jupiter is the biggest.

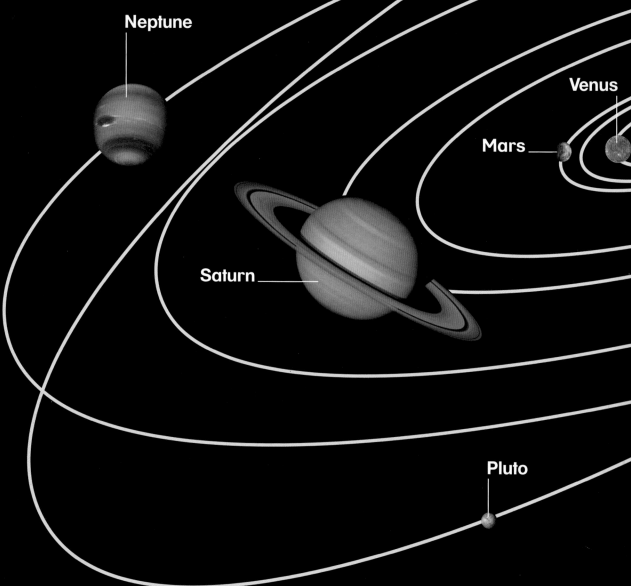

Neptune

Venus

Mars

Saturn

Pluto

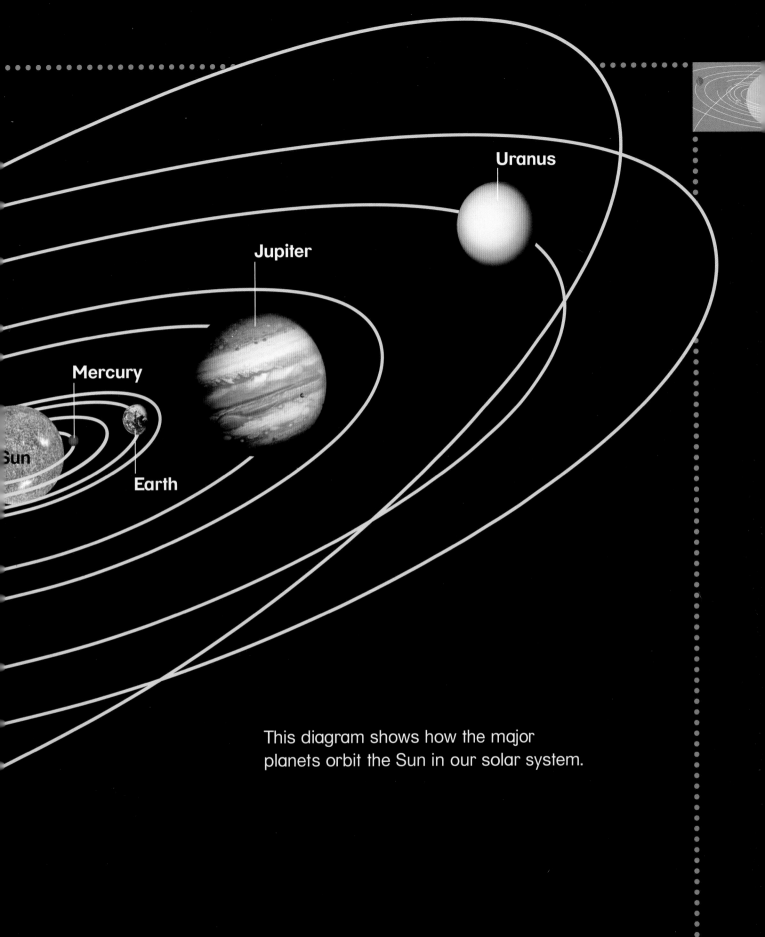

Uranus

Jupiter

Mercury

Earth

Sun

This diagram shows how the major
planets orbit the Sun in our solar system.

Exploring Space

How do people explore space?

Long ago people explored space by looking at the night sky. Today they use telescopes to help them see more clearly. Astronauts and space probes also explore space.

These telescopes on Mauna Kea, Hawaii, take pictures of space objects.

What do telescopes do?

People use telescopes to study space.
Telescopes make distant objects appear
larger and brighter. They allow people
to see far into space more clearly.
Some telescopes are used to take
pictures of planets and stars.

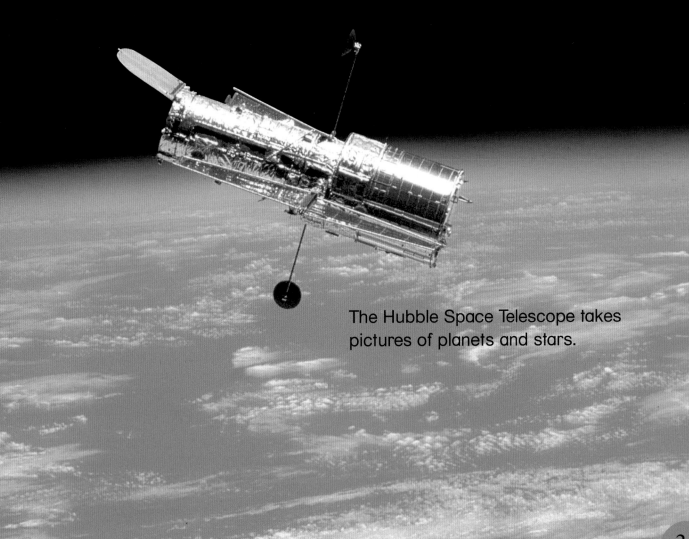

The Hubble Space Telescope takes
pictures of planets and stars.

What are space probes?

Space probes are machines that study space. They collect information and take close-up pictures that a telescope on Earth could not take.

Galileo is a space probe. It took pictures of volcanoes erupting on one of Jupiter's moons. It sent the information and pictures back to scientists on Earth.

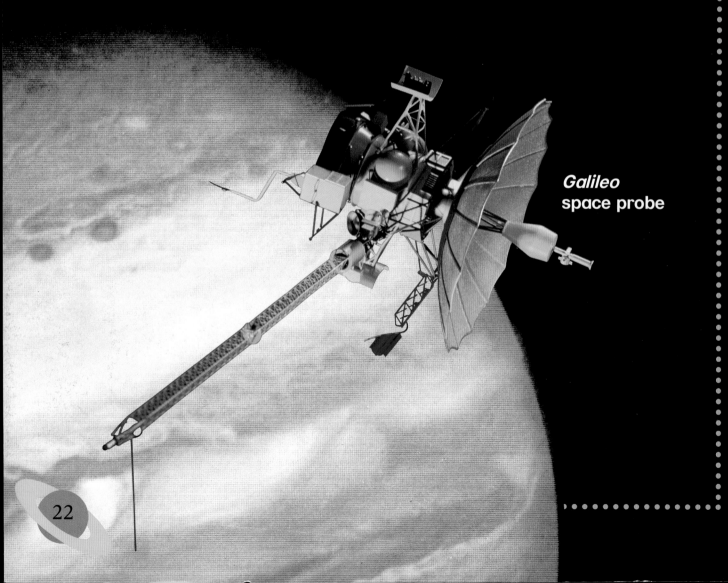

Galileo
space probe

What do astronauts do?

Astronauts make new discoveries each time they travel into space. Sometimes they repair equipment in space. Some astronauts live on space stations. Their discoveries help others learn more about space and about Earth.

astronauts working in space

A History of Space Exploration

1957 *Sputnik I* is launched. It is the first object made by humans to orbit the Earth.

1959 *Luna 2* is the first spacecraft to land on the Moon.

1961 Yuri Gagarin is the first person to travel in space. He travels once around Earth on 12th April, in a flight lasting 108 minutes.

1968 *Apollo 8* is the first spacecraft to carry astronauts around the Moon and return to Earth.

1969 On the *Apollo 11* mission, astronaut Neil Armstrong is the first person to walk on the Moon on 20th July.

1981 The Space Shuttle *Columbia* is sent into orbit around Earth. It is the first spacecraft that could be reused in space.

1990 The Space Shuttle *Discovery* takes the Hubble Space Telescope into space.

2000 The International Space Station opens in November. Astronauts and scientists from all over the world live and work on the space station.